BEARS OF THE WORLD™

PANDA BEARS

DIANA STAR HELMER

The Rosen Publishing Group's
PowerKids Press™
New York

Many thanks to Don Middleton, member of the International Bear Research and Management Association, International Wildlife Rehabilitation Council, and founder and webmaster of The Bear Den, at http://www.nature-net.com/bears/

Published in 1997 by The Rosen Publishing Group, Inc.
29 East 21st Street, New York, NY 10010

First Edition

Book Design: Danielle Primiceri

Photo Credits: Cover shots © Kit Luce/International Stock, © Joseph Van Os/Image Bank; p. 4 © Mark Newman/International Stock; p. 7 © Maratea/International Stock; p. 8 © Michele and Tom Grimm/International Stock; p. 11 © Zhi Wu Bian/Image Bank; p. 12 © Joseph Van Os/Image Bank; pp. 15, 20 © Luis Castañeda/Image Bank; p. 16 © Yi Min Hou/Image Bank; p. 19 © 1996 PhotoDisk, Inc.

Helmer, Diana Star, 1962–
    Panda bears / Diana Star Helmer.
        p.   cm. — (Bears of the World)
    Includes index.
    Summary: Refers to the debate about whether or not pandas are bears; then discusses primarily the giant panda, its habitat, food source, reproduction, and relationship with humans.
    ISBN 0-8239-5133-2
    1. Giant panda—Juvenile literature. [1. Giant panda. 2. Pandas.] I. Title. II. Series.
QL737.C214H44 1997
599.789—dc21   96-37697
    96558   CIP
                                                                                        AC

Manufactured in the United States of America

Table of Contents

Raccoon or Bear?

What animals are black and white and red all over? Pandas!

There are two kinds of pandas: giant pandas and lesser, or red, pandas. Giant pandas look like black and white bears. Lesser pandas are red. They look a lot like raccoons.

Some **scientists** (SY-en-tists) think all pandas are bears. Others think all pandas are raccoons. Still other scientists believe that pandas aren't raccoons *or* bears, and belong in a group by themselves.

In this book, we will talk mostly about giant pandas.

Many scientists think that lesser, or red, pandas are part of the raccoon family.

A Bear Like No Other

Giant pandas can grow to be six feet long and can weigh close to 300 pounds. They are as big as most black bears. Giant pandas got their name because they're bigger than the smaller "lesser" pandas.

Thick fur makes giant pandas look even bigger. Most bears are hunters. But giant pandas hardly ever hunt. They don't see very well or move very quickly like other bears do. So even though pandas are **omnivores** (AHM-nih-vorz) and eat both animals and plants, pandas mostly eat bamboo plants. Bamboo is easy to catch!

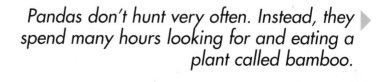

Pandas don't hunt very often. Instead, they spend many hours looking for and eating a plant called bamboo.

What Makes a Bear a Bear?

Pandas don't always act like other bears. So scientists looked inside several giant pandas to see if they really *were* bears.

All living things—even people—are made up of tiny **cells** (SEHLZ). Inside cells are **genes** (JEENZ). Genes make you a girl or a boy, a person or a panda.

Giant panda genes are like bear genes. But lesser panda genes are more like raccoon genes. Many scientists believe that the gene tests prove that the giant panda is a bear, and the lesser panda is a racoon.

Since pandas don't eat like other bears, scientists decided to take a closer look at them.

Pandas Are Puzzles

Giant pandas have always had secrets. Long ago, people hardly ever saw the giant pandas. Pandas live in the mountains of a country called **China** (CHY-nuh). Each panda lives alone, hiding in the bamboo of the mountain forests. Most days in the mountains are rainy, dark, and cold.

Pandas hide so well that the **Chinese** (chy-NEEZ) used to believe they were magic. It is also believed that no one outside China had seen a panda until 1869.

Even today, wild pandas are hard to find and watch. Scientists often have to study pandas in zoos to learn about them.

It can be hard for people to find pandas in the foggy mountains of China. ▶

Eating the Night Away

Every panda has a full-time job—eating! These omnivores eat mushrooms, mice, roots, flowers, honey, and other things. But of every 100 meals a panda eats, 99 meals are bamboo stems and leaves. Pandas have stomachs that can **digest** (dy-JEHST) tough bamboo stems.

Bamboo is a tough grass. It grows to be very tall, usually ten to twelve feet high. People use bamboo to make baskets, tables, chairs, and even houses. Imagine chewing up a table or chair. No wonder it takes pandas so long to eat!

◀ *Pandas can spend up to sixteen hours a day eating.*

Still Hungry

One panda can eat 40 pounds of bamboo a day. Yet pandas rarely get fat or full. Most of the bamboo that pandas eat goes right through their bodies. So pandas don't get much **energy** (EN-er-jee) from bamboo.

During the winter, bamboo stops growing on the mountaintops. Pandas move down the snowy mountains to find other types of food. They don't have enough body fat to **hibernate** (HY-ber-nayt) through the winter without eating the way that some bears do. Pandas stay awake all winter looking for food.

Pandas sit up to eat like people do. They hold bamboo stems and leaves with their paws while they eat. ▶

Living Alone

Each panda has its own space or **territory** (TEHR-ih-TOH-ree). That territory can be up to two miles around. A panda eats bamboo only from its own territory. In one day, a panda may eat from an area of land the size of a soccer field. Pandas stop and sleep under trees during the warmest part of the day and late at night.

Pandas like to be alone. They scratch marks in the bark of the trees around their space. They also rub an animal smell called **musk** (MUHSK) on trees and rocks. These signs tell other pandas to stay away.

Pandas tell other pandas to stay away by scratching marks into the bark of trees around their territory.

17

Single Parents

Pandas only go near each other during **mating** (MAY-ting) season. Mating season lasts from March until May. But females only want to mate for a few days during that time. After males and females mate, babies can start growing inside the females. These unborn babies don't grow much inside the mother until June or July. Then they grow quickly. They are born in August or September.

Pregnant (PREG-nunt) pandas make **dens** (DENZ) in caves or hollow trees. They fill their dens with bamboo, and sleep a lot. Usually only one bear cub is born to a mother. Every once in a while two cubs are born.

Female pandas don't like to mate very often. They prefer to be left alone.

A Bear Is Born

Newborn pandas are white and as small as chipmunks. They have no teeth, and they cannot see. One month later, these cubs look like tiny giant pandas. Mothers sometimes carry their cubs in one paw as they search for bamboo. Sometimes cubs wait in the den. **Leopards** (LEHP-erdz) and wild dogs often hunt panda cubs that are left alone. But they don't hunt grown pandas. The only **enemies** (EN-em-eez) that pandas have are people.

Panda cubs grow quickly. When they are four months old, they can ride on their mother's back. When they are about five months old, they can eat bamboo. Panda cubs leave their mothers before their second birthday.

Panda cubs stay with their mothers until they are almost two years old.

Save the Pandas

Scientists believe that there are only 1,000 giant pandas left living in the mountains of China. One hundred pandas live in zoos around the world. Pandas don't mate very often. And when they do, the cubs often die or are killed by other animals.

The Chinese are working to protect giant pandas and to give them special, safe land on which to live. Hunting giant pandas is against the law.

Many people around the world care about protecting giant pandas. They are looking for ways that pandas and people can live peacefully together.

Glossary

cell (SEHL) The basic building block of all living things.

China (CHY-nuh) A country in eastern Asia.

Chinese (chy-NEEZ) People who were born in China.

den (DEN) An animal's home.

digest (dy-JEHST) The process of changing food into energy.

enemy (EN-em-eez) Someone who doesn't like or wants to harm something or someone else.

energy (EN-er-jee) The power to move or grow.

gene (JEEN) Any one of several tiny parts joined together in a cell that make a living thing like its parents.

hibernate (HY-ber-nayt) To sleep through the winter without eating.

leopard (LEHP-erd) A large, wild, spotted cat.

mating (MAY-ting) The joining of the male and female bodies, after which the female may become pregnant.

musk (MUHSK) A liquid that an animal's body makes to mark its space.

omnivore (AHM-nih-vor) Something that eats plants and animals.

pregnant (PREG-nunt) When a female has an unborn baby inside her.

scientist (SY-en-tist) A person who studies the way things are and how they act in the universe.

territory (TEHR-ih-TOH-ree) A space that an animal or group of animals takes as its own.

Index

DATE DUE

10-2	2		
11-1	21		
GAYLORD			PRINTED IN U.S.A